M000074668

# VICTORIO'S WISDOM

## Awakening to the Spiritual Evolution

MAIRI E. R. BUDREAU

# About the Author

Mairi Budreau was born in Toronto, Ontario Canada in 1961. She grew up on a farm with four brothers and was a strong willed tomboy. She didn't feel part of the family and left home at 15 moving north to canoe country. Camping trips and working in Algonquin Provincial Park bolstered her love of the outdoors and admiration for Canadian painters, The Group of Seven, and Robert Bateman.

She did not complete high school but continued independent studies in art and literature.

Budreau married in 1983, had a daughter in 1987, and divorced in 1991, then moved to British Columbia. There, she apprenticed informally for three years with Native artist, William Kuhnley Jr. before starting a career in art.
Her works have been exhibited in New York,

London, and Vancouver. She is an AFCA, Associate Member in the Federation of Canadian Artists.

Mairi studied at Vancouver Film School graduating in 2000, and holds a diploma in graphic design 2007 from Thompson Rivers University. She has been awarded several honours in art, photography and documentary film.

Budreau married again in 2008, is Gran to two delightful boys, and lives with her beloved husband Al, and two cats in Kamloops, BC.

As for the spiritual stuff, read on...

© 2016 Mairi Budreau

All rights reserved. No part of this book may be used or
reproduced in any form without permission in writing from
Mairi Budreau, her heirs or successors; except in the case of
brief quotations embodied in critical articles and reviews.
**www.mairibudreau.com**

**email: budreau@shaw.ca**

Cover Design by Mairi Budreau Publishing and Design

Cover image Portrait of Victorio ca. 1877 Courtesy of National
Anthropological Archives, Smithsonian Institution
(negative #75-8329)

Edited by Bronwen Scott

Published by Budreau Publishing and Design


Library and Archives Canada Cataloguing in Publication
Budreau, Mairi,1961–
Victorio's Wisdom: Awakening to the Spiritual Evolution / Mairi
E. R. Budreau

ISBN 978-0-9868603-3-1
Ebook 978-0-9868603-2-4

Printed by CreateSpace

*for beautiful you*

# PREFACE

This account may challenge the beliefs of some readers through its presentation of messages from the deceased leader of the Warm Springs Apache, Victorio.

Some may have concerns that a white woman is writing about Indigenous people, and that new untruths may be added to those already recorded in history.

The intent of this book is to share information that may present healing pathways, and build bridges between cultures, and to fulfill a task prescribed to me from an enlightened spiritual being. This is a true account of my experiences expressed from the heart.

*Victorio, I hope these messages are presented in a way that fulfills your inspiration for bringing them into the world.   – Little Doe*

# VICTORIO'S WISDOM

Awakening to the Spiritual Evolution

# CATALYSTS

# CATALYSTS

Wisdom from the spirit world doesn't just arrive out of thin air, well actually it does, but without a receiver prepared for it, the messages might be misunderstood or even missed altogether. I had no clue I was being prepared for such a task.

It smacked me in the face the moment I met my spirit guide. It was the single most significant event in fifty-five years of life. My throat choked with emotion and my thoughts fell into a chasm of hazy memories, like the clarity of a dream that fades as one wakes. Instantly and intricately I knew I was related to him; my chest tightened with raw pain. At a cell level I felt I lost him along the way, triggering a flood of tears. Sobs ached to come out but other people were around so it was awkward. I felt him see me; the back and forth between us was intense. I was mesmerized by his smoky Native American eyes. Was I standing in a torn seam in the fabric of time? The sobs locked painfully into my neck and shoulders and I muscled them down into the core of my body. I broke our trance to look out a window – to focus on something else – but his face filled my mind's eye.

The unfamiliar sight of sand, cactus and disjointed Joshua trees added to the foreign feelings tumbling through me. Maybe the soft green rain forests back home in British Columbia might have felt better, but nothing in those moments could have changed what I was really feeling.

What an unreal connection! I had stepped up into the enclosed front porch of a house, and on the wall hung this portrait that must have been photographed in the 1800s. When I looked into those eyes my feelings were instantly thrown into chaos and body swamped with grief: what the hell just happened? Somehow I knew this guy, and judging by the age of the photo he probably died before my parents were even born! This was nuts! It rattled me to the core, and I wanted more. And I got more than I could ever have anticipated and I have to share it now.

I had to leave that house, but I came away with two facts about the man in the photo: his name was Victorio and he was a contemporary of Geronimo. This was enough to start researching him because I was full of questions I'd never thought of before, and I so dearly wanted to find that picture.

**The set up** for this meeting actually started organizing five years earlier, unbeknown to me. I left my home in Ontario, my marriage, family, everything and moved three thousand miles west to British Columbia. A few months later I met Dr. Karl Schutz best known as the originator and architect of the historic outdoor murals in the town of Chemainus, BC. Then I worked for Karl, and he invited me to assist him on a business trip to California. Karl was a great supporter of my art career and was about to introduce me to someone important in the art world. On the way we stopped to pick up his associate, Mary Jane Binge, and on the wall in her front porch was Victorio's picture. Some time earlier Mary Jane had been to a medium and was advised to have an image of a Native American in her home. She came across his photo at a garage sale, felt drawn to have it, paid a couple of dollars, and displayed it in the entry of her house.

I don't know for certain why the meeting happened there so far from home, but I do know that not having the photo – just the riveting memory of his face – was the catalyst to start researching. I learned a lot about Victorio before finding his picture again. Without this research none of what I'm about to tell would have ever happened.

I wondered how this intense "meeting" was going to weave into the curious symbiotic relationship I had felt toward First Nations people all my life? Since a child I yearned to live alone in the wilderness, I cheered for the Indian to win in the movies, I fantasized about living their lifestyle because they seemed in possession of supreme skills for living on the land, appeared wise and all knowing. I wanted to be one of them, fully tuned to nature and the wilderness.

As a young adult I learned how to trap and skin animals (which I could not do now), winter survival skills, and favoured canoe camping and snowshoeing over shopping for clothes or partying. What is strange to me now as I look back on this time is that I didn't educate myself about the tribes. I was satisfied with the fantasy of feeling the earth as I thought they did.

Simply by being Native American, Victorio fit into this Indigenous fantasy world, but the emotions he stirred were new. There was something personal about this. How could I have actually known him? Why did he appear? Why did my feelings twist into a hurricane? How did I lose him? Were we once a couple or siblings? Had he made it into history books or did his look of "an Apache type" simply catch the eye of a photographer, dead-ending any chance to find out more about him?

I could barely wait to get home and scan for his name in the index of every book I owned about Native people. My little library by this time probably held fifty books, mostly about the Coastal tribes of BC. There was one mention he was Apache – but I already knew that! Then I scoured the Internet and found he was a leader, a warrior who died in battle, he was a Coppermines, Chienne, Mimbres, Warm Springs, Chiricahua Apache. These names made no sense to me at the time, except for the name Chiricahua, attached to Geronimo, the last holdout of the Apache wars. Search after search, the picture of Victorio remained illusive. Two years later, I was walking out of a bookstore and the name 'Geronimo' ambushed me. I spun on my heel and pulled a little orange book from the shelf and fanned through the pages. The picture of Victorio was there, and so were my emotions! If I hadn't known he and Geronimo were contemporaries, I may not have even noticed the book.

Obviously, researching history would not answer or explain why I felt emotionally attached to Victorio, so I turned to other means: a friend who was also a medium, Patricia Gunn. I had a psychic reading with her in 1992 when she was beginning her practice, then I moved away and we lost touch with each other. I remember an Indian came through in

*Victorio*
Leader of the Warm Springs Apache
circa. 1877 Courtesy of National Anthropological Archives,
Smithsonian Institution (negative #75-8329)

that reading so long ago and I thought she might be able to contact Victorio and get some answers to my growing list of questions. In the interim years, Patricia became a fully-fledged medium and ordained reverend of the Cowichan Spiritualist Church of Healing and Light.

**Mediums** have varying abilities to see, hear, feel, and read symbols, and through one or a combination of these abilities they interpret information in a conversational manner. Mediums access spirits by raising their energy. Since everything is energy they can link into the frequency matching that of spirits, like tuning a radio.

And then there are channelers who can write, speak, paint, dance, create music, or engage in other creative forms through which the channeled information can be expressed. To channel, one allows the energy of spirit to occupy the body. The source of the information comes from the Collective Consciousness, and the personality delivering it from the other side is a spirit entity, a guide, an ascended being, or spiritual master. Channeled information is concise because it doesn't rely on interpretation by the medium.

In 2001, Patricia and I first communicated with Victorio. It was conversational, and he said I was his granddaughter. Wow! Really?

It's common for deceased grandparents to reach out to younger generations; the only thing was my paternal grandparents were born in Ukraine, and my maternal set were Canadian from French and British heritage. I was born and raised white Canadian; Victorio was Apache; how could he be my grandfather? How did this connection exist, and how was I able to feel it with no prior knowledge?

But that wasn't all, then he explained he was my spirit guide, a spirit who before I was born agreed to work with and look out for me while I walk the earth; who nudges my thoughts, gives impulses to go here, or look there, and provides many other signs that I will hopefully clue into; all to help me accomplish what I set out to learn and grow from in this lifetime.

I learned that some spirits guide our entire lives while others attend to us for shorter periods of time. Several guides with specialties help us pass through different stages or hardships. Everyone has guides whether they believe in them or not. They aren't puppeteers, but can help when allowed to do so. They especially want to help in challenging times but cannot force their way in. Guides use many ways to get our attention, but it's up to us to learn the language of their signs, and means of contact. The simplest way is to just invite them in! There are agreements too, made with other souls who show up in the life journey.

**On July 14,** 1996 Victorio had already been in spirit 116 years before he got in my 35-year-old face. Perhaps when I was born we said goodbye, and the 'finality' of that ending is what swept over me when I saw him. I do know Victorio is my guide for life. From what I've learned so far, it's a rare occurrence for a spirit guide to appear in a photograph.

**In my early** years some things took place suggesting I had access to realms beyond regular everyday life. I saw the ghost of my grandmother after her funeral when I was ten years old, three years later a disturbing prophetic dream tragically came true, and still later I smelled my deceased uncle's pipe tobacco while sitting with his wife, who was about to pass away. From age six I could sense illness in other people and by the time I was twenty I could listen to a diagnosis and know if the illness would be fatal. I didn't see these events as forecasters of a spiritual life or being prepared for a task serving the spirit world. In fact they were unsettling and caused a lot of anxiety. They happened and life went on. But they did overrule what I was taught to believe about life and death. These experiences proved to me that people and animals didn't die; just their bodies perished. Where their life energy went afterward and how it all worked was a big fat mystery to me, but one I was genuinely curious to understand.

So after that first reading when I learned Victorio was my Grandfather and spirit guide, there was a fair bit to wrap my head around because I didn't know about all this spiritual stuff or how it worked. I looked for proof of the grandfather connection and it was startling and amazing to find lots of sound, convincing evidence. It's not relevant to include that paradigm-shifting story here, but later.

There was more to discover about Victorio so I bought and read every book I could find that looked promising. I learned there were several branches of Apache people. I studied their ethnology, sociology, mythology, and language and scoured for precise information about Victorio's era; where he lived, how he lived, his descendants, and his death. I tracked down private military journals that mentioned him, and even found his name in census records. The Internet grew and a greater abundance of information about Victorio became available, even books with his name in the title.

Everything I read about him was cast in a shadow of war between the Apache and US forces. Biases, ignorance, violence and injustices came from both sides and always ended with Apache freedom being caged when they became prisoners of war.

The history lay heavily on my chest; it felt so personal. I dragged an empathic heart through reams of horror stories of what Victorio, leader of the Warm Springs, lived through at the leading edge of Manifest Destiny. Manifest Destiny was a widely held belief in the United States that it's settlers were destined to expand and dominate across North America. After a decade of reading, I felt for and supported the Apache side one hundred percent. I was angry about the exploitation of a brilliant yet illiterate society whose way of life, when not at war, was in many ways more spiritually advanced, ethical and humane than that of those aimed to oppress it.

All that I had read was baked into my head, but I had to see and connect with it in person, so I drove alone seventeen hundred miles from Canada to New Mexico, to let my hand drift in the warm springs of Victorio's homeland. I walked where he lived and travelled, saw the land he fought so hard to keep free for his people, and was moved beyond words to spend an afternoon with the oldest of Victorio's living relatives, the last prisoner of war alive.

*Budreau at Ojo Caliente, New Mexico 2005*

**A few years** later I had a reading with Patricia when I was coming out of a difficult period with my health. The whole session was about past lives. I didn't request it, in fact I didn't even know she could access past life information, but it was obvious the guides wanted me to see that these lives were connected to my ill health. In two of them, I was Apache, an overly aggressive warrior and my recklessness killed me off in battle at a young age, and the other was the granddaughter life that Victorio referred to, and she lived during the period of assimilation into white society. Learning about these Indigenous lives made sense and I marinated in the juicy feeling that I was an orphan finding my birth family.

**Victorio has 'spoken'** at every reading over the past fifteen years. Each reading was recorded on cassette tape, DVD, or video and took place either in person, or over the phone. I always felt inspired, refreshed and supported after a reading, but as the weeks and months passed the details softened, the impact subsided and rarely did I replay them. The early readings were conversational, grandfatherly, humorous and personal. Later, as my research about the Apaches deepened, Victorio expressed opinions about the pain felt by modern Apaches with suggestions to help them move past it. Then the tone of the messages shifted into advice for The People and the delivery went from conversational to direct spirit channeling. I will not forget the first time it happened; the tenor of the room changed, I felt it, and then Patricia's voice deepened slightly, and her speech went from conversational to monotone in an even, measured pace. When he finished speaking he 'stepped back' from her and she expressed relief it was done. She wasn't fond of him 'stepping in' like that, because he was very powerful, but allowed it.

Ever year Victorio brought forward that writing a book was on my to-do list, and other guides mentioned it too. He said it would be about truth and Native people, but I didn't have information like that, nor did I know how to obtain it, so I doubted the book would ever be written. True, there were lots of interesting encounters with Victorio and spiritual activity in my life to write about, but those were not a story on their own. Besides I was a busy artist painting portraits. But then things took an unnerving turn and in the span of a few weeks my inspiration dried up and I was in artist hell, under the pressure of completing a lucrative commission, and organizing a big solo exhibition with no desire to paint. I was confused by the sudden evaporation of desire and how I would live up to my professional standards, follow through on my word, and hold up my portion of household finances – but the impulse to write this story about Victorio gushed into my mind like high tide.

So I finished the commission, cancelled the exhibition, dropped all painting plans and disappeared from peers and social media. I pulled out the collection of recordings and played back forty plus hours of readings then spent days transcribing them. Something quite unexpected happened while transcribing: other ideas slipped in, richer meanings and realizations emerged and a wave crashed into my brain, and then I saw it, *Oh My God, what have I got here?* Clearly Victorio's messages are about an evolution that is unknown, information about humanity that could make positive changes in the lives of many people. Now I know what it is they want me to write about.

I sifted through journals, sketchbooks, and photos; read over dream diaries, reflected on old artworks, and dots started connecting between the macrocosm and the microcosm of what I learned. Epiphanies unhinged my jaw nearly everyday and oh my, did tears of wonder flow.

Awash with information and inspiration, I wrote about Victorio and my kinship to Indigenous people, and that led into the art career and reached back to a childhood brush with death that later bled into decades of anxiety and depression that almost ended my life. Three hundred pages with lots of woo woo spiritual stuff, it turned into my biography – not what I intended! Three themes emerged but I couldn't see a way to tear them into separate stories, so I lay the manuscript down and put my mind onto other projects that I made public. They were rich in growth but financially fruitless, cosmic jokes, I suppose! I licked my wounds then clarity came and I chopped and boiled and dissected the biography down to Victorio's Wisdom.

**What I learned** about Victorio as a warrior in the 1800s compared to my experience with him as a benevolent spirit with compassion for all humanity, is pretty remarkable. I want to share some of what I learned about him so anyone can see the gulf of change he crossed.

The Apaches were a nomadic culture living in present-day southern Arizona and New Mexico. It's likely that Victorio was born near Ojo Caliente,

New Mexico, around 1820. His Apache name was Bi-duyé. There is no record that his was a family producing a succession of leaders, but in the Apache Way if you speak up, demonstrate wisdom, show respect and contribute to the health and welfare of the group, you become a leader. Victorio became a highly respected leader among the Warm Springs Apaches, a branch of the Chiricahua.

The role of leader was partly democratic; he sought out opinions from those also well respected before making decisions for the welfare of all. The other part was personal sovereignty, operating out of one's own sense of governance; a guiding principle. As long as his decisions served the higher good of the group, dissolved disputes within the camp, maintained relationships with other camps, led to successful hunting grounds and raids to support their needs, and he remained a fearless warrior and defender, a leader retained the position. If he fell out of favour he was replaced. If he grew too old he simply stepped back, perhaps mentoring a replacement who wasn't necessarily kin.

Before the time of the warpath of the 1850s, Victorio mentored under the leadership of Cochise and Mangas Coloradas. Mangas was murdered and dismembered in 1863 by US soldiers at Fort MacLane, New Mexico, and Cochise died in 1874, probably of cancer. Victorio, and Nana, an older warrior, led the Warm Springs.

At this time the Apaches had been tolerant of mining as long as the white men would leave as promised, but welcomes were overstayed, distrust and betrayals erupted and people killed on both sides. Into this fray the Mexicans introduced scalping for cash (learned from the Spaniards) which was adopted by the Americans who added alcohol, smallpox, and weapons.

There was plenty of confusing double talk from the white man, sparking skirmishes and surprise attacks amid steady pressure to move Apaches off their homeland. Women, children, and babies were being killed; it became obvious to Victorio they were facing extermination. In spite of these hardships and challenges he wanted peace; he spoke of

CATALYSTS

it; he negotiated for it.

By 1876 the warpath was a horrible way of life. They had to fight to survive. They lived in constant readiness to defend, kill, escape, or die. The people became worn down and hungry so Victorio tried the white way. He was willing if it would bring peace, but he would not surrender his freedom. His people walked 300 miles from Ojo Caliente to San Carlos, Arizona, where deplorable conditions met the weakened and weary families. Scorching heat, biting insects and the broken promise of food proved the white way was not for the Apaches. To stay alive they escaped and made it back to their homeland.

Twice during Victorio's life the US ran a military outpost at Ojo Caliente, attempting to control and teach them how to give up the nomadic life by growing crops. He had been captured once in 1877 (probably when his picture was taken) and rumours abounded once more that he was a wanted man. Remembering what happened to Mangas, he kept his distance from the whites, sending scouts to deliver his negotiations rather than walking into a trap.

The American settlers continued moving west, farmers took more and more land, miners sought rich veins of copper, silver and gold that lay beneath the land the Apache called home, while the US Military was defining a border with Mexico that cut through the heart of Apache land. All arms were pointed at them; they were seen as an obstacle in the way of Manifest Destiny.

Trust had been broken many times and was hard to rebuild even though attempts were made but failed because of actions on both sides. Apache numbers grew small, many great warriors were dead and babies did not live long on the run. Life was little more than grave.

It took just over twenty-five years to cut down a race of people that for centuries had thrived on an unforgiving desert and rugged forested mountains. They were tough, lean and hardened with exemplary stamina and ingenuity in warfare, but they had never encountered an enemy as psychologically inhumane as the white man.

Telling a lie was an incomprehensible act: a liar was severely punished by exclusion from the group; was sent away to die. The punishment was severe because false words could threaten Apache survival, and each person was key to the survival of the whole. They believed the white man's words –at first.

Another bewildering concept was land ownership; it was incomprehensible to them because the land was the Mother, the provider, a spirit with a temperament respected because she supported all life and communicated with the medicine people. She could not be owned. Yes, it's true tribes 'held' territories for hunting and resources, but they were not holdings that could be bought or sold.

Apache 'ownership' looked like this: objects used in daily life such as clothing, baskets, horses or a shaman's talismans were treated with reverence. These objects held the energy of the person who used them. When someone died, the items used by that person were destroyed, buried, or permanently damaged so no one living would use them, even accidentally. For the "one who was gone" there was nothing left for the ghost to cling to. The spirit was free to go into the next life with the things carried in this life. Kin didn't fight each other for things used by the deceased, nor did they inherit anything, in fact they did not accumulate belongings. Memories could hold you in the past, and keep ghosts around. As a rule they would not say the name of the departed ever again; if it were necessary they would say, *the mother of so and so.* The Apaches owned nothing, yet everything was available to them.

Surrounding and supporting their culture were elements beyond their control, like the weather, the stars, and Yusen the Creator. These elements were spiritual powers. The land was part of this power group, sacred and honoured for her gifts of sustenance, medicine, shelter, beauty and teaching. The stars gave direction and were a constant from which their shamans accessed knowledge and guidance. And as with all nations, they had a Creation story, theirs featured Yusen.

In 1879 Victorio returned home from hunting and saw the US military had visited Ojo Caliente. He found his wife and mother murdered along with many women and children of his camp. Their deaths wiped out his desire for peace; the loss too great, too direct a hit. Victorio rampaged against the whites for the rest of his life. History called this time the "Victorio Wars." His military genius, elusive escapes and almost magical maneuvering earned him high respect from legions of the US military that pursued, but never caught him.

The precise end of Victorio's life remains unclear. General Joaquin Terrazas of Mexico and his men cornered Victorio with several warriors and a battle erupted. The Mexicans claim they killed him, but the Apache survivors said Victorio committed suicide, an accepted practice to prevent the humiliation of becoming a prisoner. He was about sixty years old. No matter how he came to take his last breath, Victorio died in the Tres Castillo Mountains of northern Mexico on October 14, 1880.

Victorio's life had been drawn into a race war with a conquering society and he was on the losing side. Six years after his death, his descendants became prisoners of war.

Loaded into freight cars they rode for days to Florida, where the men were disembarked then ferried to Fort Pickens on Pensacola Island, and the women and children were railed another three hundred miles further to St. Augustine. All were locked up and many died in the thick, humid climate from malaria, tuberculosis, small pox and homesickness.

After a year, the survivors were reunited and moved to an army barracks in Alabama for the next eight years, then moved to Fort Sill, Oklahoma, were they remained prisoners for another eighteen years. Their children were shipped off to schools for assimilation into the white way.

In 1913 after twenty-seven years, freedom came,

but the Warm Springs people could not move back home. Ojo Caliente was privately owned. They were given the option to stay in Oklahoma and be free or move to the Mescalero Apache Reservation in New Mexico. Some moved, some stayed.

Today most Apaches live a fully modern lifestyle, but the stereotype of savage, wild killers depicted in movies and history books lingers with their name. But in truth they are beautiful, strong, resilient, gentle people.

Several generations have come and gone since removal from their homeland and they feel the torn fabric of their culture, the lost stories, the lost medicine traditions, and miss the elders who flowed with spirit food from the ancestors. Many have adjusted and many still carry a collective pain from the warpath and assimilation days. Many modern Apaches are caught up in this pain of the past and have difficulty moving forward with their lives. This is this pain that Victorio wants to ease.

# WHY A WHITE WOMAN?

# WHY A WHITE WOMAN?

Why did Victorio choose me, such an unlikely messenger for the dissemination of his wisdom instead of a modern Apache?

He made it clear he wanted someone with distance from the pain but who could also understand it. He compared my struggles with Apache struggles. Now that seems like quite a stretch. How could a white Canadian woman, middle class, have struggled, even remotely, like the Apaches?

The first part of the answer comes from my past lives: the reckless warrior who died young, named Roaring Bear, and the granddaughter who was part of the first generation to be assimilated. But there were other Indigenous lives, too. A young female Navajo in the 1700s who died bleeding out after childbirth, another as a medicine woman in Canyon de Chelly, Arizona, trying to keep people alive during a drought. In the 1600s there was another life as a medicine woman, tribal counsellor and high-ranking wife from the Eerie tribe of the Eastern Woodlands. Also an Algonquin life, a male loner hunter born in the 1450s in the days of first contact. These lives refer back to one of Victorio's first comments in the very first reading, *"One aspect of your soul has re-incarnated in the Native World."*

I saw that woven into my soul were the credentials of what it was to be Indigenous, plus an experience of assimilation.

Learning about these lives was like waking up from amnesia. They confirmed the intense empathy I felt for what happened in the past, plus the symbiotic relationship with Indigenous people. The common ground between me and Victorio appeared solid.

And Victorio explained the second part of the answer, in my current life I was raised in a white family and spared from growing up with a history of pain.

Thankful to be spared that, it didn't however limit any attachment to Indigenous people, the traditions, values, or fervent connection to the land. Imprints of these past lives were all just beneath the surface of my white skin.

**Moving to Vancouver** Island, BC in 1991 was an act of courage and freedom; I knew one person in the whole province and I wanted a new start.

On this beautiful emerald island I discovered many First Nations people living there. To me it was like heaven seeing them in my daily travels and I wound up loving and working with an Aboriginal carver for three years. This relationship brought me face to face with the impact of colonialism on First Nations people. I saw chronic family dysfunction on the reservations. I looked into the vacant eyes of so many lost souls of young and old people grieving for a way of life that worked for them. I saw garbage and rusted-out vehicles piled in their yards and concluded, "*yes indeed, we whites have successfully assimilated you, you disrespect the land just like us.*" It tore a strip off me. The Canadian history I learned in school taught me a one-sided romantic pioneering tale. My naive notions about pioneers and Indian life were shattered.

I felt these Coastal people were my people, my family, not lost causes, not to be left in the back corner of Canada's closet. They were the descendants of thousands before them who were whipped through a radically accelerated time machine from hunting and gathering to the 20th century industrial age. I sunk deep inside a dark pit to feel what that would be like. They were stripped of rights, land, sovereignty, even the freedom to feed themselves and handed alcohol to numb feelings and memories, and they were abused by a religion and the bringers of it, that burrowed deep into their souls altering ancient beliefs. British culture dominated and exploited them, carted off their children for indoctrination into the white way. The economic ocean of the Coastal culture, the Potlatch, was turned into a criminal offence. It was all so horribly incomprehensible to me and twisted my soul into knots. I entered an extended period of inconsolable grief.

Three years later a purpose grew from the grief in the form of giving back. I wanted to pour back to them all that had been taken and more. I wanted to honour and pay respects to all Aboriginal people, to hold up their beauty, truth and wisdom and their high example of companion living with the land for all to see. I acted out of emotion and every First Nations person I met or passed on the street I gave as much warmth through my eyes and smile as I could give. These wants of giving came out in my art, journaling, soul searching and writing to newspapers.

But I didn't feel I was really helping. The problems seemed too complicated and the numbers of people were daunting, how could I even begin to convey my compassion for their suffering? How could compassion possibly help them? I saw my white skin as a huge obstacle. I assumed and feared they would see me as "one of them, part of the problem." My sensitivities for sensing illness and predicting death kept me away from direct contact on the reservations. I had all these feelings to work and sort through. A path was not clear but the desire to search for ways to change the relationship between whites and Indigenous peoples remained at the forefront of my thoughts.

And it changed me. I felt attached to Aboriginal people and not my birth family or the white society I lived in. Without realizing it, there was a nationality switch. I felt home with "the Indians"; these people were me, I was them. The book *Ni-Kso-Ko-Wa Blackfoot Spirituality, Traditions, Values and Beliefs* by Long Standing Bear Chief has an explanation fitting my experience,

"... a person is not an Indian by blood only. I could have been raised in Africa or Germany. Culturally I would be an African or German and love everything about being who I was raised to be. A person learns his or her culture and traditions. You do not automatically gain a culture just because you are born into parents of a particular culture. Race does not play a part in determining who or what you are."

When this nationality change happened I didn't know about my past lives, I didn't know about

Victorio or spirit guides; it was a pure response to instincts.

Even though my new allegiance was clear, it presented a struggle that I would wrestle with for more than two decades. On the Aboriginal side of me was grief, sorrow, compassion and an overwhelming desire to heal the wounds of my people and to inspire whites to see the importance of an apology and allow First Nations all the freedoms that fulfill their needs and aspirations.

And as a white I witnessed their pain feeling wholly guilty and responsible for the atrocities. I was part of the ignorant society. I was born into it and participated in it. I was inextricably ashamed of the greed and arrogance of my white forefathers. I was overwrought about the acts of oppression, the lack of respect, the lack of help from citizens and governments. I was appalled by the systemic disdain for the drunk Indian passed out in the alley, by how whites, including me, were oblivious to our role in bringing on these hardships.

At the time, I often compared the two societies and a favourite analogy is this: among Coastal tribes, they housed even the lowliest man or woman in the village. There was a place for them inside the long house; it was by the door, drafty and cold perhaps, but indoors, fed and with others. In white society, the lowliest people are homeless, no family, no shelter, no support, or quality food. It was plain to me which culture was more civilized.

Friends tried to convince me it wasn't my pain, wasn't my fight and wasn't my fault, but I was up to my eyeballs in the injustice of injustices. I empathized with the betrayals suffered by Indigenous nations of the America's, it had no end for me until it was solved in some form.

This struggle in me is what Victorio saw comparable to the Apache struggle.

**When I inhaled** books about the wars he was involved in, and when accounts were inaccurate or were biased in some way, Victorio helped me get at the truth by impressing corrections in my mind as I read. He wrote the truth into my thoughts and zero time elapsed between what I read and his corrections instantly popping in. Later, in readings, he confirmed he was helping me learn the truth of the history.

And the research had an unexpected outcome. It helped Victorio, and others in spirit, advance in their growth. I was shocked to hear research was helping him. It didn't seem possible, but numerous times the readings spoke about how our deeds are connected with spirits and there is a reciprocal arrangement.

Victorio explained the research was filtered through my white worldview and allowed me to empathize with, but not be bogged down by, although it was close sometimes, the Apache pain collective.

A pain collective was explained by Eckhart Tolle in *A New Earth*:
"The pain-body, however is not just individual in nature. It also partakes of the pain suffered

by countless humans throughout the history of humanity, which is a history of continuous tribal warfare, of enslavement, pillage, rape, torture, and other forms of violence. This pain still lives in the psyche of humanity and is being added to on a daily basis..."

I suppose we inherit degrees of pain from the families we are born to. It may be that my Ukrainian bloodline passed down pain because great aunts and uncles were shipped to Siberia during the Russian Revolution and never returned. There is so much we do not know about the energy of these physical bodies we live in and the soul energy we bring into them.

The research helped Victorio evolve on the other side and its evident in the readings that he advanced from a grandfather and spirit guide to a higher-level being bringing peace at a world level and beyond.

Isn't this amazing: warrior to peacemaker, this is the gulf of change he has crossed.

I have often thought, *"you never know the full impact of your actions,"* but I never ever considered it could have an affect in the spirit world. In Sara Wiseman's, *Your Psychic Child,* a passage from The Messages says, "This is not the only world you are in; this is not the only work you are doing." How profoundly we affect one another, how thin the veil between us and spirit.

I was curious to know the mechanics of the spirit world and specifically about this spirit guide relationship, how could a man who killed become a spirit guide? This question came up while reading about Victorio's rampages. Could I be vulnerable to some psychic harm? Patricia gave an intricate and insightful explanation that is included later in this account.

**For twenty years** I've been grateful Victorio got in my face on a scorching day in southern California and that he had the courage to take me on for this life journey, because I've never fit the mold, it's not been easy, I can be intense and demanding of details and assurance.

I have come to learn Victorio is a spirit with access to rarified levels of new information for humanity to navigate and accelerate soul growth through the spiritual evolution. What a gift.

**Below are excerpts** from readings with Victorio, showing his support and guidance to make this information available.

## 2001 – First Reading

PATRICIA: He agreed to work with you before you came here. I don't know what you believe about past lives, but it goes back [in time], he wants to call you, *Little Granddaughter, Little Doe.*

VICTORIO: *One aspect of your soul has re-incarnated in the Native World. You wanted to come [into this life] as part of your soul work and bring out the truth about Native Culture. It required someone who is "not Native" to have the distance to put it in perspective and bring balance. You honour past traditions. You're not caught up in the pain as so many First Nations people now are. They can't get beyond that.*

## 2002

PATRICIA: He's quite an eloquent speaker, quite an intelligent being. He says, *we often bring [into this life] the residual of past experiences [past lives], this part of our expression of being. This is why you are drawn into the Native culture like a magnet.*

## 2004

PATRICIA: He gives you thoughts of wisdom. When you sit in meditation or go for walks, have a notebook with you because you may get fragments of a sentence, or a thought. You don't always retain them but keep a little notebook and write them down.

He says, *we can continue them if you write them, if you try to remember it blocks the next. Don't try to do this, just allow it to happen.*

If you start to get a thought that you feel is beautiful, write it down, you might get more when you get home.

VICTORIO: *We've been giving you these gems. It's part of your art, you have to write it down, Little Girl.*

PATRICIA: He's patting you on the back.

So there is a mix of facts and misinformation that you will see [in your research] but he will give you insights.

He says, *we know the people like facts,* but he will give you insights, words, to express really who he is, getting the essence of him.

VICTORIO: *The book will be a balanced account of First Nations. You're not First Nations, you have the outside view so it's more likely to be balanced than somebody writing who is First Nations protecting it or slanting it. You're going to be led to get the truth, an objective truth. This is going to take many years, it may be two to three years or ten years,* he's not saying, it's not going to happen overnight.

## 2005

VICTORIO: *We go with you wherever you go.*

He means, those in spirit who are walking with you, and he will walk with you your entire life's journey.

*VICTORIO: We honour and respect your search for truth – understand the people.*

## 2007

PATRICIA: He's not pressuring you, but there's still a desire to see you accomplish the story. You'll get impulses to follow a track, or write something down or sketch something and then your own busy life will come in and that is fine. But he would like to see it done at some point. He doesn't want you to feel pressure.

*VICTORIO: They [The People] have to find a way to know that preserving history is preserving the past – but it is the past – take what is good, add it and leave the rest as the story, the story of growth. Somehow you'll play a part in bringing some of this to light.*

## 2008

*VICTORIO: We honour you for what you've done – it's been part of your growth because you've had to look at things and see the realities of what went on in the early days. Reading is still helping you to learn. You've been a hard working little girl. I thank you on behalf of my people on the groundwork you did, the research you did.*

MAIRI: I'd like to ask about people who kill. Victorio murdered people, so how does a soul with that kind of history come to deliver healing messages?

PATRICIA: I've asked about that kind of thing, I have asked about Adolph Hitler, what was the intent behind the intent? I've asked about soldiers too and what comes back is: not every soldier wants to go out and kill somebody. They were either drafted or found themselves in a war defending their country. The intent to kill really isn't in most soldiers. Some do relish the violence, but for most it's to protect; they've gone to war with the good intent to protect, but they will feel the effects of their actions for sometime. When they pass over they will have a life review like everybody does, and see the effects of their actions, but it is also balanced by the positive things they have done.

Victorio killed to protect his family. Nobody is saying stand there and let your family or tribe be killed. A lot depends on the motive behind it – the intent, the real intent – not the surface excuse.

MAIRI: I've been wondering how he, a man who did violent acts, could be my spirit guide? Can he harm me?

PATRICIA: He's been over there for some time – he's had a soul review, he's learned. Sometimes being a guide is the way they earn themselves into a higher light. He isn't your only guide, he's one of them, and perhaps you're helping him, because it's always a two-way street.

As guides, they want to earn 'Brownie points' by looking out after us. So we're helping their soul grow in a sense. They live vicariously through us because they are influencing us and if we're following through and something positive comes from it – then yes, it works. In a sense you're helping him by doing the research about the Apaches.

He says, *no one is blemish free. We've all done and said things that we're not proud of.*

They point out that when we've done things that we're not very proud of, we look back and say, "I don't feel very good about that. I don't want to feel like this again. I don't want to hurt anybody else." So when that type of situation comes up and we are aware of our behaviour and try not to repeat those words or actions, instead responding from a point of love or compassion, then we move forward. When the situations happen again and we find we're reacting more from our heart in a positive way, that is not hurtful to other people, all of that is soul growth through life experiences. That is what we are here for, soul growth. We come into this life with things we have to learn and how we learn them is being put in situations where we have the choice of how we're going to react. Nobody is expecting anybody to be reacting perfectly from day one.

Warriors and soldiers in wars today may think they are bringing peace to save their country, some get disillusioned, they are not happy when they come back home and don't ever want to go back; while other's feel its their duty. They reap what they sow.

WHY A WHITE WOMAN?

A lot of them feel so sick when they return home and need a lot of counselling to put what they did or witnessed into perspective. If they don't get the counselling in this lifetime, they will get it on the other side in their soul review, they will be helped to put it into perspective then. Today they have choices about signing up for the service. Knowing full well it can take them into battle and they might have to take someone else's life.

Maybe that's part of their journey, maybe they need to experience that. That was pointed out to me when I asked somebody in trance about Hitler. The guide that was channeled said, "Who are you to judge Hitler? You do not know his real motive behind what he did – you don't know the situation leading up to it and if was it part of his soul's journey to be the catalyst for a war. In many ways that war woke up a lot of people to a lot of things in spite of the great injustices that were done, and yes, they were horrific. We don't know what his soul journey was to accomplish; maybe that was it. You put that on top of the heap of the worst things.

Take people who murder; when you read the backstory of how it came to be you can understand sometimes why they kill. Then you take it further; that person chose that environment and that family to be born into to learn something. But who are we to say they learned it well, or incorrectly?

MAIRI: And then there is the ripple effect.

PATRICIA: And the killer gets to feel that during the soul examination. There are Wise Souls who help them. They don't take away from the effects of what was done, but help to bring a full understanding of the big picture to the person responsible.

A lot of people in spirit actually want to make up for something they've done if they can, and they may be a guiding influence, even for a short time, with somebody connected to their family. You see, a whole family may be sent in a destructive direction because of something someone has done in the past that affects them today. A spirit guide may want to even out some of the energy from the situation by encouraging somebody to change their way of thinking, or their direction away from drugs or obesity, and get them into a positive light. That's spirit's way of making amends.

We're told, the more knowledge we have of this the more responsibility we have to act with spiritual maturity. That is our journey, to learn to react to life with spiritual maturity. Some of us are slow learners and some of us have been born into volatile situations.

So Victorio is your guide earning Brownie points working with you, and no, he will not harm you.

### 2009

PATRICIA: There's a whole group of them [here] and I think they are connected with Victorio because they are saying, *Thanks for the interest you have shown, and for your desire for the truth to present the Apaches as people and not wild savages.*

It's not Victorio saying this, it's a lady, I don't know who she is. They're all called Grandmother over there and she's thanking you for searching out the truth. The fact that you took the interest – they are thankful to you – because there's so much misperception. When people take the time to see beyond the myths and to see the Apaches as people, and even if only a few get the information, it's somehow uplifting; it's healing something. I don't know what you're doing, or what you've done with the book, or if you talk to people about it, but it's going to heal on two levels. It will help some people on earth and bring healing for some of them in spirit. It's getting some truth out there.

They're not pushing you to hurry. There's a feeling that you will know how to do this when the time is right. Somebody is going to inspire you with a thought. You know when they were talking about getting a clear vision, thoughts and answers? The present time isn't quite right to do it. I don't know if there are more facts to be found. You're going to be given help with this. It will just happen. A huge bulk of the work is done – it will happen.

They're all [the band of First Nations people on the other side] such a protective force, an inspirational force and will always be there as part of your team. They are grateful you've followed that inner drive to do what you've done so far. At some point, they're not giving any clue as to when, this book will happen. Sometimes they have to work to get the right people to bump into each other. In the meantime they're asking you to enjoy yourself, just relax, they say you've earned your happiness, but there's a lot of work for you to do yet.

## 2011

VICTORIO: *Nothing you did was wasted. In some ways all this research you did has been helpful to us as well as you, but you've done enough.*

PATRICIA: It's important you understand there was an aspect of your soul that had some incarnations as First Nations and so it was partly for your healing for your soul to do this.

VICTORIO: *Each moment is precious and live it. We cannot alter the past.*
*It was.*
*It is good to honour the true facts of injustices, but*

*they were, they are not now.*

*It is your job to live fully and honour your soul, your presence here. By creating light and harmony in your existence you bring beauty into the world with your art and your presence and that is enough. The exploration of the First Nations that you got so focused on for a while was part of your journey. Your job is done.*

PATRICIA: You needed to do that for you as much as anyone else.

MAIRI: I know it's done, I feel that, and I am sad, its left a big vacuum.

PATRICIA: I don't know why it was therapeutic to you, maybe on some soul level it did something for you, healed something.

He says, *you don't have to do it anymore.*

It doesn't mean he's running away, he loves you. That journey has brought you to where you are at the present, he just keeps saying, Live, go forward and spread your light, but send thoughts of healing and love to First Nations."

# VICTORIO'S WISDOM

# VICTORIO'S WISDOM

**What** follows is Victorio's wisdom written without a filter. His thoughts are not cleansed, softened, nor made politically correct. His choice of words may seem harsh, controversial or to some, just the right tone. They have been edited in small ways for clarity and to clean out jargon. The channeled messages are word for word.

Patricia and I are messengers only: here are the readings.

### 2001

*I hurt for the lost souls of my People. I also want to kick butt. There's so much potential mixed up. It can't all be blamed on the white man, some yes, but not all. I see all nations co-existing, enhancing, respecting nature – everything.*

*You've got to take on the responsibilities of your life.*

*There are some First Nations people who won't be happy about what we're saying. We would like to give some of them a swift kick. We're not happy with the whiners that are sitting feeling sorry for themselves, they didn't go through a lot of this (wars and atrocities) and they are not making the most of their abilities. Some of them are using it as an excuse.*

## 2002

*In this lifetime Little Doe, you chose not to be First Nations, as you call it these days.*

PATRICIA: He's laughing about being politically correct.

He says, *we were called a lot of things – mostly derogatory.* That's an unusual expression from a First Nations person.

He's laughing and says, *remember, we had other lifetimes in other cultures too, don't lump us into one category.*

PATRICIA: That's the first time any of them have brought that up; always a first. He's looking at life from both sides.

He says, *there was a lot of shame on both sides, the white man and the Natives; we weren't perfect either.*

He's showing me two-handedness.

*Some of us were not honourable in our dealings and some of the whites were not honourable. When we get to the other side we see in spirit, just people. You people (on earth) still can't get that.*

*Many of them [First Nations] are looking to regain self-respect but they don't treat themselves with respect. It has nothing to do with white culture. They have to recognize they have to be respectful of themselves and their culture before others will do the same. They're sitting on their laurels of self-pity, but not all of them. It's being passed down generation to generation, so respect is going down. For them to function fully, it really has nothing to do with any other culture, but themselves. They don't see that yet.*

*Each human being that shows The People respect, plants seeds of self-respect. You, Little Doe, are interacting by doing those pencil drawings, you're showing respect and it triggers something within the other Natives who see the drawings. Like, who is that? What was their story? Why would somebody do that? Why are they being honoured? Because for you to draw, there is honour in that. For you to draw totem poles honours and respects those that created totem poles. You're somebody white who is honouring them. Then they turn it around, if somebody outside honours us, maybe we should look at ourselves as to what there is to honour?*

## 2003

*Truly, in spirit we don't have nationality here.*

## 2004

PATRICIA: Victorio wants you to sit, he's taking you down to the river and he's showing life's logjams, and the rapids, and everything it creates. When you feel you've hit a logjam, remember to let the water flow. If you can't see an answer go to the river, go into nature, let the river of life flow until the clarity comes to you as to whether you are to do something or not to do something.

*Art Thompson*
Nuu-Chah-Nulth artist
Close up
1995

*Chief Walter Harris*
Gitskan artist
1995

*Simon Charlie*
Khowutzen Salish artist
1994

*Grizzly Totem Pole of Tanu,* Haida
2/3 scale replica drawing
with Mairi Budreau
Photo: Ulli Steltzer 1998

VICTORIO'S WISDOM

He's stressing, *there are times when it's just a log-jam, a waiting period, but if you remain quiet and don't panic about it you will be able to just let it clear on its own.*

*Stay at peace so you can see clearly whether or not you need to move. We will let you know when and how to move. Sometimes the power of the river moves the logjam, you feel you're just treading water. Stop and enjoy it instead of fighting it. You look and see if you can do anything. If you can't, then stop and recharge your batteries, go do something else.*

## 2005

PATRICIA: Victorio, the very powerful native is here. He is happy with your continued interest in things that are Native.

He's laughing, *what you would politically call First Nations.* He thinks this politically correct stuff is nonsense. *You are who you are. The name doesn't matter, although, we were first!*

*Many of my kind forget there are many good people who are non-Native. There needs to be a blending – just people. To be proud of your heritage is one thing, to dwell only on the wrongs done creates bitterness, despair and anger. It is time to mend the wounds, to become as one nation. We respect those who search out the truth – recommend the idea of one brotherhood.*

*Those of us who have spent much time here in spirit have learned the ways of war do not bring peace; they bring more dissension and disharmony. It is a difficult conundrum for your people to find the ways to bridge the gap. But both sides in many instances are defensive towards one another and fearful of the unknown. On both sides many are caught up in wrong perceptions of God who created all nations as one; all nations to be equal.*

*Spirituality is of the soul, of respecting the earth, the sun, the moon, and the sky and all Creation, and all Creation includes mankind. This is not what you expected to hear, but I feel compelled to share my understanding of what I have come to know here. You see, even I am continuing to learn, to understand.*

*It is difficult with so many unruly people on earth,*

*so many stuck in their opinions, but there are many like you who try to understand the history and the deeper meaning.*

*The earth and nature were created by the same who created all people, creating a place where your souls can be nurtured, grow and experience.*

*The problem of defacing the earth comes from all nations, all colours, and all beliefs. All are defacing the earth. That has nothing to do with religious beliefs, it has to do with souls that are angry souls, that are frustrated souls, that have not been taught to respect the earth in all its beauties and gifts.*

*Your thoughts and your interactions with other people are also powerful. We cannot change people in one sweeping motion; it is one mindset at a time, as the souls respond.*

## 2006

Victorio says, *when I was alive, starting the day would begin by holding my hands open and up to the sky giving thanks to the Great Spirit. There was a ceremony we did in the morning; it's almost a cleansing, but a spiritual cleansing and welcoming in the day.*

PATRICIA: He was a peaceful man in his heart. He wanted what was best for his people. He had to do some things that were distasteful to him. He was trying to protect his people.

He says, *I am sad that so many of my people have lost their way and I'm glad that some of the younger people are beginning to respect the older ways. And I'm glad that some of the stories are being shared because the whole story needs to be heard. I know it will never be the same, but what I hope for is a peaceful blending of people.*

*Having people from the outside, such as you, who are white – even though there is a soul connection – it is important to have people like you be born and have that interest in the First Nations. These are steps in the right direction to show there can be a blending, of letting barriers down.*

*There are individuals doing this all over the world,*

*and it is good to have quite a few of these mixed couples. Even though it appears to cause problems, the children are important steps in the spiritual evolution. It appears to be backward steps sometimes because of the confusion of two cultures blending, but in actual fact, it is the beginning of stepping forward. To step forward there is always confusion. Confusion before clarity. It isn't a bad thing, but look at the pattern, not only of First Nations but of all nations, nationalities in a melting pot.*

MAIRI: Canada is a melting pot of nations.

PATRICIA: Yes, and he's saying, *all over the world there are those who will be staunchly rebelling against cultural blending, but the younger people are looking beneath the surface of colour. Even if they look for the richness of their heritages they are seeing the similarities [between all people] and then are mixing, it's good.*
*The [blending] steps also create confusion because it has happened in a relatively short space of time. It's also important to keep the richness of the different heritages by preserving the textures of the culture.*

*Show the truth of each culture, the beauty in each culture, through each truth. The purpose of preserving the truth of each culture is to show the diversity of creativity, the beauty and the growth.*

PATRICIA: Now he's going beyond First Nations, he's showing me Africa and India and all these different cultures from Mexico and South America, all having beauty in their own cultures. And it's the richness of each one that adds to the tapestry of life.

*In the future they will look back and see the oneness and the separateness at the same time, something that is beautiful. It's not right now. It seems to be happening at some levels, but in others, the fear of blending is the fear of losing the history. They have to find a way of knowing that preserving history is preserving the past – but it is the past – take what is good from it, add it, and leave the rest as the story, the story of growth.*

*We don't stay in the past in the spirit world, otherwise we'd be stuck, in spirit we become aware of new possibilities.*

He's laughing, *you haven't seen everything – yet. We know possibilities you don't know of, we're not sitting around philosophizing all the time!*

PATRICIA: Even though he's connected with you, he works trying to influence some of the remnants of his people. He's trying to influence them in a positive way partly because he'll be able to bring about some of the information that you search for. He links with them within their energy field and tries to get a thought into their heads. That's how spirit get us to places; they influence us to turn right instead of left and go into that little coffee shop and sit next to that person, that kind of thing.

And he says, *remember there is no day or night for those of us in spirit. We have lots of time and energy to work not only in the spirit world, but, to link with various people here on earth. There is a plan, but we don't tell you the whole plan on purpose because you have to deal with what's happening in the moment and live your life as fully as you can.*

*There is diversity in friendships, and diversity in things. The greater purpose is the souls development and that means having friends of all nationalities. Remember the Oneness, experience different facets of life and different cultures, allow them to unfold into the bigger picture. Just allow it to be, it's all unfolding just as it should.*

## 2008

PATRICIA: He's talking about his own people:

*We want to pick some of them up and shake them. They're too mired in past grievances to move forward. I was a forward-looking man when I was here and some of them have forgotten that. Instead of moving forward into the 21st century some of them are holding onto grievances from the past and some are like horses with blinders on, they can't balance. They're just focused on how hard done by they were, not how things are now in the present day. If they would take the blinders off they would see new possibilities by honouring the past and moving forward into the present. They are holding themselves back and it makes me very sad.*

*They think they honour the past by staying focused*

*on old wrongs. We would like them to see the truth through the past, honour it and then take respon- sibility for making the most of their abilities in the present.*

PATRICIA: He's showing me a picture now of all the different nations of the world holding hands.

He says, *if you could only get people to recognize that. I have grown a lot in my greater spiritual understanding. I continue to grow, and I honour your growth, Little Girl, you have expanded your horizons.*

*I would like to shake up some of The People and yet I know their situations are difficult. I see the greater picture now; the earth is one large family and in amongst my own people there is still infighting, so how can they accept other nations when they can't move beyond themselves?*

*And this is why it's good to travel to other countries as well as back in history. It's the history of mankind. You haven't learned anything – it's still happening but in a different sense now.*

## 2011

*We're so sad there's so much infighting among The People. They have to work that out themselves with thoughts of love and healing and let it go. Thoughts of love and healing are what will help. There is a soul evolution for each particular nation. It's part of a soul evolvement for the whole group. This evolution is part of something they're working out, and they have to work it out. For others who had soul journeys in it, who lacked tolerance, they are their own worst enemies. We say this with love.*

*In some ways we find this modern world fascinating but then...*

He's showing me where there were beautiful forests and now there are smelly cities. He understands people need homes and the world has grown, but it makes him a little sad. Where he is, he can have it the way he wants it.

*It's sad that some people never get to experience the great outdoors. Not that they can't, but they spend their whole time in these boxes and some never know nature is there except through pictures. And*

*then they go on tour buses, only seeing nature as a
huge group instead of on their own.*

He's sitting by himself on a hill, being at peace and
at one.

*As a group they don't get any of that silence because
there's too many people around. But that is their life.
But you know, Little Doe, that you and I love it.*

PATRICIA: It's interesting... I watched him start
walking away and his First Nations clothing just
disappeared and he's wearing robes. He has
evolved as a soul and I can see his silver robes. He
can put the leather on as recognition for you, but
he's telling me, *one nation, there's no division, no
division, now I'm free.*

PATRICIA: I believe he's showing me he's moved
up; he's evolved on the other side. Robes of pure
light and he's of no one nation, he just is, because
the robe is loose luminous colours.

*This is where I am,* he says.

PATRICIA: Whatever your research did, it helped
him. Whether it was bringing into focus some

event or whether you were a catalyst in some way you don't even know about. There are other things involved, but, he's free.

He says, *our soul journey never ends.* And he's now moved on. He has a faint interest in earth now, not as closely connected, but the connection to you will always be there. He's moved even higher into a spiritual place where his focus is a broader spiritual growth, all encompassing, and still he is always sending love to his people to encourage them, but they have to sort themselves out. So he blankets the whole world; this means he's moved on to a higher plane now.

## 2015

MAIRI: Victorio has spoken about the Spiritual Evolution of nations: the blending of cultures through assimilation, mixed marriages, slavery; is there anything else he wants to say about it?

*The process has begun already if you look around you. In many countries there has been amongst the younger people an assimilation of marrying into different cultures so there are what you call "the mixed race children" and for them, as this continues to happen, colour and race will be less important, but right now the world is in a place of confusion.*

*For often, you understand, that for the greater change to happen there is turmoil underneath where those who do not want change resist and create turmoil or wars. There are those souls that are digging in their heels, resisting, they have forgotten that there is one Creator that created all. They have forgotten that there are many aspects of that Creator and that all are good, that none are superior to the other; that all of life is part and parcel and necessary to the other, so at the moment the world is going through the turmoil.*

*There are some countries in Europe as well as Canada that are assimilating people who are fleeing the terrors of war, where they are trying to assimilate many, many, races to understand that we are all alike.*

*We are born, we love and are loved, and we get hurt.*

*We care about our families and our friends and it does not matter what colour you are, what race you are. The basic personalities, the basic characteristics of all people are the same. It does not matter what they look like on the outside. It does not matter how they worship the Creator, it only matters how they treat one another.*

*Some areas of your world are more open to that, but there are other areas where fear and intolerance are strong. There is fear and intolerance in all areas of the world but in some places it is stronger and that is the danger.*

*But always remember that the Creator is the one in charge. The Creator has given the world free will, but does not desire to see the world destroyed and will not allow that to happen. But yes, there are years more of turmoil where those in power for the most part, or in a large area, will fight the assimilation, but they will be the losers in the long run. Those who recognize with compassion and humanity that people are just people, that they are part of the family, those are the areas that will thrive and they will prevail and the children of those countries, they are the new leaders for they will understand it doesn't matter what nationality their parents were, they are loved. And so they will love those who do not necessarily look like them.*

*Do not allow the fear of those in other countries or even within your own country to take over your mind or your soul. Encourage the love of differences within the children and the grandchildren. Teach them we are one family and send love to all those area where there is fear and where there is war and even in the smallest circumstances of your own areas where the children, the grandchildren, maybe involved in gangs or trying to control others. Teach them to love, not to harm.*

*It starts at home. It starts with your communities showing compassion and tolerance for that which is different. Teach them right from wrong, and teach them compassion.*

*The world still has a long way to go, but there has been much growth. It is just that your newspapers, your internet emphasize the negative. Within that, there are always bright souls that are caring and compassionate. It is learning to let go of the fear of differences, that is the key.*

*You are a light in your world. When you create wells of beauty with words or in paintings then you stimulate the souls and the minds of others to seek for the beauty and to understand the oneness of all life.*

*I will always touch your life although I may not always be in the forefront. You are part of the greater family, as such, I am aware of your path, so I leave you with love. May the Great Spirit walk with you.*

# RIPPLE EFFECTS

# RIPPLE EFFECTS

The spirit of Victorio nudged me to write this account, and what I've learned has taken effect.

His influence has redrawn the map of my past; answered some questions about the Great Mystery, turned my behaviour upside down and literally inside out.

It's apparent now that the highest purpose is found in relationships, not careers; the idea of nationhood is blowing away; forever I am changed.

And I had no idea researching a relationship with him was going to inform me of a spiritual evolution.

He said, "We respect those who seek out the truth." To find some truth to this relationship with Victorio turned me into a researcher of history, the mechanics of spirituality, and the science of the quantum field. Curiosity led me to drink from the fountains of master teachings from different cultures and the consistent theme in all of them is: we are all one and we are here to evolve.

Long before I understood this, Victorio said, *"Spirituality is of the soul, of respecting the earth, the sun, the moon, and the sky and all Creation, and all Creation includes mankind. This is not what you expected to hear..."*
He was right, hearing that Creation includes humankind actually bewildered me because what I saw was an ugly divorce between people and nature: the earth being sued for every last bit of value, and no longer receiving tender loving care or respect from her partner.

Often I wept in the wilderness for what nature has suffered at our hands. I have been underwhelmed with the 'respect' humanity has shown. More and more people seem disconnected and have become more fearful because they don't know, or even try to understand her nature. We may be in the midst of losing the privilege to live on such a beautiful planet. If we are included in Creation, how do we reconnect?

I'm not blind to the caring people working tirelessly to preserve and protect nature from further damage–some even put their lives on the line—and many Indigenous people thankfully remain close to the earth and valiantly protest to keep areas intact. These saviours are worthy of admiration. They are nothing short of honourable and courageous in their heartfelt and future-minded acts. But they are a small group.

The big group, the majority of people in the western world, arrange their everyday lives around business, home, school, children, and capitalism; nature is way down the list. For many, nature is in the way of short-sighted goals. Some people cut down a mature shade-giving tree because it's too much work to rake leaves in the fall. Some wake up grumpy in the morning because birds are singing and some dump their garbage at the side of a road. These are not horrific acts compared to what industry does, but they are everyday signs of disconnection.

The industrial age and the capitalist frenzy has fed off a belief system based on separation. The separation paradigm is old and is fortunately falling apart because of what is being learned about matter, energy and space, in other words, quantum physics. Everything is connected, everything is inter-related, and everything is energy. Separation is an illusion we have come to believe. Science is backing up the Oneness. Science and spirituality are twinning in the language of Quantum. This is a great time to be alive!

Paradigm shattering experiments show that thought energy affects everything, so to go about our lives thinking we are separate from an enemy, a flower, a rock, a blood cell, a star, the air we breathe, or a departed relative, is false. The Indigenous people have always know this. We have long believed we are separate from everything, or fear being separated from people and things; is it any wonder conflict appears most everywhere! Through understanding this entanglement of the base atomic structure of the Universe I was able to reconnect humanity to Creation.

**Victorio recommended a** spiritual practice. What would that involve? It took a couple of years to get going because I had all kinds of excuses: the biggest one was not enough time to slow down.

I started by using oracle cards for guidance, then balancing the chakras—energy centres in the body. I read dozens of books, from *Black Elk Speaks* and *The Upanishads* to Einstein's thoughts, and I consistently meditated. More than two years of "being still" has changed my thinking and the well being of my body. I have authentic thoughts guiding decisions, my purpose has become clear, and excitedly I accept the real me who has come out from under the pile of crap I refer to as "What Others Demeaned Me To Be." Hurts buried deep from long ago are still dissolving. I behave using less mind and more heart, and the list of changes goes on.

Ironically, at the start, meditation caused me fear

because the spacey feelings triggered anxiety. I did it anyway, in small increments. After about a year, meditation flat-lined the anxiety and it no longer rules or cripples my life. Now I meditate for an hour and love the spacey feelings!

**For a long** time, I felt I was in the wrong skin and looked down on the white race I was born to. Victorio said it's important to blend cultures, and to let down barriers. I didn't see myself as racist, but in a weird twisted way I was prejudiced against my own culture. The division between loving and hating myself nearly brought me to a psychological breakdown in 1997. I could not sustain both views and be healthy, but I didn't know Victorio's wisdom back then, so more mental and physical health problems would hit me later.

Victorio said he had other lifetimes in other cultures, and Patricia's readings revealed the same of me. In addition to several Indigenous ones I had past lives in England, Spain, India, and Egypt, so I reasoned there is an accumulation of multi cultural experiences being held in the history bank of my

*Bloodlines*
Victorio, Budreau, and her Ukrainian Ancestor
Photo montage 2004

soul. I carry the energy of other races and traditions and ideologies into this life. Knowing that energy cannot be created or lost, only transferred, I deduced the beliefs and traditions of all those societies were functioning peacefully within the soul that presently is me.

In this account of Victorio's Wisdom I favoured the Indigenous side. That bias has fallen away; the wall between my white self and Indigenous self has disintegrated because I come from where there are no nations and no divisions, yet I live in a body extracted from many nations: at least six bloodlines.

I accept my body and soul self as is and occassionally sense its lineage and imagine millions of fibres spreading back into many cultures—truly a wonder.
I can't find a single situation to support racist, separatist views.

**Nature never fails** to show the connection of bird to tree, tree to earth, and so on: the interconnectedness of all life. Encounters with people show the same kind of connections. Each person I meet is a welcomed presenter of choices; no matter what behaviour comes, there is a choice of what to feel and how to respond to it, not just externally, but internally, and situations have navigation choices too, in full awareness of being responsible in a role in the spiritual evolution of our species.

I admit, it's challenging, I'm not used to thinking this way—it takes steady self-observation to find balance, to see innocence in people who kill, scream their own children into submission, or abuse animals. It takes looking beyond the behaviour, avoiding the ingrained impulse to judge and separate them from me. I know we are part of each other, and their part is in a lot of pain. No one who fully loves him or herself would do harm, period.

It takes setting aside judgments to see they are in a lot of pain and unaware of the spirit they actually are. Their beautiful souls are just behind the behaviour and in need of peace, acceptance and love. But if they receive judgment, it adds separation and fear, and if they receive punishment it hurts and hardens them even more.

When I've caused pain and was treated with love in return, it was a wonder.

More and more I'm seeing beautiful souls and less of the behaviour. It's fascinating how easily thoughts can go into the well-worn rut of old reactions and then be popped out and transformed into balanced peaceful energy. Plenty of times I've plowed into the ditch, pulled back out and aimed again for the horizon ahead.

**Victorio affected my** attachment to the past too. "Take the best of the past and leave the rest behind." I ached for my Indigenous family, and thought I was honouring and respecting them for what they endured. The people who lived during the warpath years were alive in my heart. But the fact I was ignoring was that these events were over, and more importantly, these people were no longer suffering. I was suffering on their behalf and twinned it to the pain of their relatives.

Was it doing any good? Did it mean I should remain feeling like this for the rest of my life? What would my sustained empathy bring into this world of energy? The answers were, no, no and pain; it would reinforce and grow pain.

Did this serve me? In part, yes, because it exposed the rewards of the Victorio research and in part, no, because holding this pain interfered with the purpose of my life.

Did it serve those who I ached for? No, not in the long run, because Victorio's descendants wouldn't benefit from what I felt. Indigenous people weren't aware of my experiences either, and the worst part was that it added to their pain collective. It was serving no one.

I had to narrow down these facts to understand what I was holding on to in my attachment to the past. I realized any prolonged negative idea playing over and over in my mind and heart extended out to others; I had to stop and refocus on the best of the best.

But then I wondered, if I stop dwelling on the sufferings of departed love ones does it mean I have abandoned them? They have moved on— where is the abandonment?

Those in spirit feel our attachment to their pain. In some instances, it is their spirits urging us to stop hanging on, to stop letting the past overpower life right now.

It became obvious a prolonged state of empathy was a misuse of the emotion; a hand burns on a hot stove and snaps away, but we keep holding our emotions over the flame.
Pain isn't a place, but a guide to find its opposite.

Reflecting back on my life turned up some baggage from other lifetimes. I had a strong dislike of Mexicans when I was a child growing up in white rural Ontario. This made no sense! It probably came from my Apache lives, and held no relevance, so I changed the feeling through accepting it as a remnant, and with a little forgiveness and replacing the dislike with acceptance, it dissipated. The key is be my own change master, keeping my house clean, so-to-speak. Only I am able change me.

With the idea of race dissolving, so too, the idea of nations fade and the need for boundaries and countries. I see us as the Earth family. I continue growing a feeling toward all people with the same oneness and connection that has endured in me toward Indigenous people. To feel less will not serve the evolution.

**Victorio pointed out** that many cultural encounters have resulted in war because they happened quickly and without awareness of the spiritual evolution - we have it now.

This part of the Great Mystery moves out to meet us and more peace-filled transitions may take place. Some souls, indeed, some countries, are already doing it, Canada is one and I am thankful to live in this accepting country. Others are not there yet—but that is the evolution—it happens in stages in the field of time, not everywhere at once.

**Spiritual evolution has** completely changed my interpretation of the US–Apache conflicts. Victorio wanted peace but his vision did not align with the conquering race. When negotiation was no longer an option he led the fight to save family and freedoms. At the same time, waves of Americans were imposing their will on Indigenous people, possibly an impulse driven by the evolution. The blending of cultures was going to happen and will continue to happen, but the opportunity to do it peacefully was lost. No one person or group rallied enough people together, or perhaps no one saw the bigger picture of the evolution that was taking place.

It is noteworthy that there are diaries written by men who were in these conflicts, whose hearts bled on the pages the truth of what they saw being harmed, and how it could be done differently. These soldiers did not rise above the force that brought them to these battlegrounds but their records are sure signs the connection to the Oneness was present. Had their hearts overpowered their minds and altered the course of their country, the United States could have expanded in harmony with a race that would have brought checks and balances to keep safe the natural world. And who knows, it could have spared the belief that a gun should be in the hand of every civilian.

It didn't have to be so ugly, so cruel and cause so much long-term damage.

The era of an eye for an eye no longer serves.

"...the ways of war do not bring peace; they bring more dissension and disharmony."

**Finally, about evolution**: Darwin's theory explains the adaptation of our bodies through natural selection, but the term "spiritual evolution" is new. A search did not pull up specifics or books about it, nor an understanding of how it applies to the tug-of-war of human history, but the collection of readings delivered from Victorio present a concert of wisdom.

There is a divine purpose behind the blending of cultures throughout time, but pain, war, and hardships come from an ignorance about the purpose to be here; and free will directed by the mind, not the heart, needs to be reversed.

**Victorio lifted me** out of the blood-soaked earth into the stratosphere for this view of what happened to Indigenous people in North America and it changed everything. I saw there were greater forces at work, not just land and resource-hungry settlers, but universal laws that pulled these nations into each other, to meet, to learn, to accept, presenting a chance for the umpteenth time.

Spirit must've been hopeful in the beginning, when Columbus called The People *Indios,* meaning: with God. How did that get missed in the history books? The Europeans respected the Indigenous people for a time, but then greed gushed in like a rip-roaring torrent, spilling blood all over the land.

Since we cause the cycle of fight, conquer, and oppress, we also have the choice not to. People can lead with their hearts. An unimaginably gentle experience of blending could occur almost imperceptibly—to explain how would fill another book.

Our spiritual evolution is inevitable as far as I can see, and no longer do we have to go blindly forward unguided. The meaning of 'as above, so below' is that as there is no division in the spirit world; so too there is none on earth. To believe we are separated from each other is the biggest misunderstanding we share and it needn't be shared at all.

**Spiritual evolution is** being brought to our attention now because enough time has passed for us to find it for ourselves, and as Victorio rightly says, "*You people on earth just aren't getting it.*"

These are some of the ways Victorio's wisdom has affected me.

Long Standing Bear Chief, wrote in 1992,
"It is impossible to be free of influence from other cultures. The traditional Indian in today's society must balance between two cultures. Many people think that this is impossible, but it is possible to be a multi-cultural person."

Like perfume, this wisdom can't be put back in the bottle. Where will we go from here?

May you feel love and peaceful intentions
May this wisdom reach you through any dark
after-effects of assimilation, slavery, racism,
oppression or apathy
and
inspire awakening
and action.

May the knowledge create calm in your heart
inspire compassion for yourself
and others
dissolve differences
and set you free of the past.

May the differences and wounds disappear
through forgiveness.
This is soul growth, what we are here for,
nothing else
for all people living in this world
across all time.
We are one.

Mairi

# ABOUT THE MEDIUM

Answers to Reverend Patricia Gunn's spiritual questions started in 1966 while she was living in London. While there, she had the good fortune to observe and listen to some of the world's greatest mediums and study Spiritualism for six more years, before returning to Canada.

Patricia joined a Spiritualist church in Toronto and began developing her mediumistic gifts. She also began working on the church platform and practising spiritual healing.

In 1978 she moved to Vancouver, BC and joined the International Spiritual Alliance in New Westminster. Top British mediums worked there and helped Patricia further her training.

In time, she was invited onto their board of directors and eventually trained as a minister. Patricia led development circles, taught workshops and worked on the platforms of several of the churches in the lower mainland. She also continued taking classes with other ministers and visiting mediums for five years before being ordained as a minister.

Moving to Duncan in 1991, Patricia and her husband Ian decided to open a Church for Spiritualism which has flourished ever since. Ian passed in 1993.

Patricia taught evening courses on Psychic/Spiritual Awareness at Malaspina College for three years, until her church workload grew larger.

Because a medium's gifts are constantly unfolding, Patricia continues to study from visiting mediums and occasionally travels to the Arthur Findlay Spiritualist College at Stansted, England, to upgrade her skills and learn different ways of working. Aside from being a minister and medium, Patricia's great joy comes from teaching others to unfold their own gifts and find their own connection with the Spirit world and personal connections to their own personal God.

Patricia Gunn is available for questions about spiritual and psychic happenings, spiritual counselling, spiritual healing, private readings, weddings, funerals or memorial services,
and naming services.

**e-mail: patriciais@shaw.ca**

# To Write to the Author

If you wish to contact the author or would like more information about this book, visit her website:
**www.mairibudreau.com/victorios-wisdom.html** for images and artwork related to this book.
or write to: **budreau@shaw.ca**

Mairi will appreciate hearing from you and learning of your enjoyment of her story and how it has helped you.
There is no guarantee that the author will reply to every letter written, but all will be read.

# Notes

Notes